BEAST

Pascale Petit was born in Paris, grew up in France and Wales and lives in Cornwall. She is of French, Welsh, and Indian heritage. Her ninth collection, *Beast* (Bloodaxe Books, 2025), a Poetry Book Society Recommendation, won an Arthur Welton Award from the Society of Authors while in progress. Her eighth collection, *Tiger Girl* (2020), won an RSL Literature Matters Award while in progress, and a poem from the book won the 2020 Keats-Shelley Poetry Prize. *Tiger Girl* was shortlisted for the 2020 Forward Prize for Best Collection and for the English language poetry category for Wales Book of the Year. Her seventh collection *Mama Amazonica* (Bloodaxe Books, 2017), a Poetry Book Society Choice, won the RSL Ondaatje Prize, the inaugural Laurel Prize, and was shortlisted for the Roehampton Poetry Prize.

She published six earlier collections, four of which were shortlisted for the T.S. Eliot Prize, most recently, her sixth collection, *Fauverie* (Seren, 2014). A portfolio of poems from that book won the 2013 Manchester Poetry Prize. Her fifth collection, *What the Water Gave Me: Poems after Frida Kahlo*, published by Seren in 2010, was shortlisted for both the T.S. Eliot Prize and Wales Book of the Year. Her novel, *My Hummingbird Father*, was published by Salt in 2024.

Petit received a Cholmondeley Award from the Society of Authors in 2015, and was the chair of the judges for the 2015 T.S. Eliot Prize. She was appointed as a Fellow of the Royal Society of Literature in 2018. Her books have been translated into Spanish, Chinese, Serbian and French. She is widely travelled in the Peruvian and Venezuelan Amazon, China, Kazakhstan, Nepal, Mexico and India. Trained as a sculptor at the Royal College of Art, she spent the first part of her life as a visual artist.

PASCALE PETIT

Beast

BLOODAXE BOOKS

Copyright © Pascale Petit 2025

ISBN: 978 1 78037 737 7

First published 2025 by
Bloodaxe Books Ltd,
Eastburn,
South Park,
Hexham,
Northumberland NE46 1BS.

www.bloodaxebooks.com

For further information about Bloodaxe titles
please visit our website and join our mailing list
or write to the above address for a catalogue.

LEGAL NOTICE

All rights reserved. No part of this book may be
reproduced, stored in a retrieval system, or
transmitted in any form, or by any means, electronic,
mechanical, photocopying, recording or otherwise,
without prior written permission from Bloodaxe Books Ltd.

Requests to publish work from this book
must be sent to Bloodaxe Books Ltd.

Pascale Petit has asserted her right under
Section 77 of the Copyright, Designs and Patents Act 1988
to be identified as the author of this work.

Cover design: Neil Astley & Pamela Robertson-Pearce.

Printed in Great Britain by Bell & Bain Limited, 303 Burnfield Road,
Thornliebank, Glasgow G46 7UQ, Scotland, on acid-free paper
sourced from mills with FSC chain of custody certification.

CONTENTS

I. **Amazonia**

10 The River
12 Oxbow Lake
14 Catfish
15 House of Puberty
17 Concert for Motherhood
18 Dumbo Octopus
19 Monkey Muriel
20 My Book of the Dead
22 Portrait of My Mother at Six Weeks
23 Maman
24 Western Façade
25 Skinner
26 Hummer
27 The Lover's Bed
29 Kisser
30 The Insect Father
31 To a Botfly
32 The Pelts of Animals
34 Pale-winged Trumpeters
35 Vial

II. **The Camargue and Languedoc**

38 On Longing
40 The Lammergeier Daughter
41 Civet de Cerf
42 Papa Guêpier
43 Choker
44 After visiting the Museum of Doors, Pézenas,
46 The Frozen Zoo
48 Bac du Sauvage
49 Ode to Causse Méjean with Takhi Horses
50 Chemin des Rainettes

51	The Beast of Vaccarès
53	Courses Camarguaises
54	The Tarasque Tattoo
56	Camargue Bull at Dusk
58	Hide (Emperors and Egrets)
60	Ode to the Camargue
62	Hide (Mosquitoes)
64	Hide (My Birth)
65	Letter to Muriel
69	The Walnut Tree
70	Maman Argiope
72	Hide (Red Crayfish Claws and a Glossy Ibis)
73	My Mother's Provençal Dress

III. Tala Zone

76	Tala Zone

IV. What Rough Beast?

85	I asked if I could leave the Earth
86	A Mother Sings
87	What Eagle Saw
88	Butcherbirds
89	Salt Bride
90	Beauty

V. Beast of Bodmin

93	The Moor Horses
95	Galloway Bull at the Waterhole
96	Roebuck
98	Ode to a Cornish Hedge
100	Song Thrush
102	Swallows
104	Murmurations at Roughtor
105	Beast of Bodmin

111	ACKNOWLEDGEMENTS

I

Amazonia

The River

started to flow when I was thirteen –
it grew between me and my mother.
I saw the jaguar bathe in the shallows.
The caiman with his crown of horseflies
accepted me as a friend.
He led me to the swift centre
where night hawks roosted on driftwood,
raised their sleepy eyelids, and were not
angered by my presence.
They were forest-dreaming
as the current took me in its arms
and whispered encouragement.
My mother's chair seemed further away
on the far bank and I could no longer
hear the words that stung. The river
glittered with waves and each
was a picture I could paint
or a book I could write. It was
as if I'd entered a new element
and could breathe water. My feet
touched the bottom where stones
told me their stories and I listened.
Capybaras barked a welcome
and even the cowbirds on their backs
gurgled as they plucked botflies
from their mounts. I plunged
into the fertile world and swam to safety.
I wrapped each wave around my neck
like a shawl of sunlight.
The anaconda swam with me
and every scale was a make-up mirror
telling me I wasn't ugly.

My brown eyes were not cowshit
but clean as the harpy eagle's,
morphos drank my tears
and fluttered on my lashes –
everywhere I looked I saw my future
was gilded blue. My black hair
mother had cropped to my scalp
grew into ringlets of vines
on which jacamars and tanagers perched.
Marmosets played in the coils and made me laugh.
When I floated on my back,
my breasts were two turtles drying
their shells on a mudbank.
And when the jaguar dived beneath me
and lifted me up into the light
I clung to his back and rode my life.

Oxbow Lake

I praise my mother's waters patrolled by piranhas,
their flanks glittering with gold flakes –

she was only warning me of the dangers of the world.
I praise the vampire fish, all four feet of him,

his sabre fangs, for he eats piranhas, just as one
big worry will eclipse smaller ones.

I praise the horned screamers perched
above her oxbow lake, their ghostly screams

preceding a storm, and the hoatzins crouched on overhangs,
their hoarse calls like nervous coughs –

their parents were only concerned their claw-
winged chicks might fall into the pool below,

where a caiman lurked, his snout nudging waterlilies.
I praise the giant river otters that made their dens

in her banks, how they worked like a family of troubles
when the jaguar paddled too close, biting him

until the water foamed red. I praise her jaguar-devouring
waters where my hand and foot buds grew

but wanted to shrink back into my trunk, my eyes that tried
to squeeze back into my brain.

For my days and nights are haunted by those otters.
For the vampire fish still surges from the depths.

For her carnivorous flesh flashed with fireflies
as the piranhas thrashed faster and faster, until the surface

churned with that feeding frenzy I call my birth.

Catfish

My mother's face looms over me – a giant catfish
        shattering outside my incubator, hundred-eyed and gilled,

her body gashed by my birth. She is followed
        by a spectacled caiman, his snout deep inside

her torso, like a hand inside a puppet. I think
        he is my father, my glass box reflected on his glasses.

Doctors and nurses perch on bleached branches
        toppled in drifts by storms. The consultant is a king vulture,

his wattle a stethoscope. I know this place from
        my mother's interior, her bleeding colours, the semi-dark

like the sky just before a storm, gusts whipping me
        as I was borne on a river of detritus swept from her forest,

tree trunks and birds' nests adrift.
        The water is boiling glass, the incubator my raft

which swirls in eddies, whirlpools, stirring more caimans
        from the mud, which glide past me, eyes clustered

with butterflies – a kaleidoscope of fluttering wings.
        An anaconda is clasped to my mouth, oxygen

pumps through it, as it once pumped into my belly
        through my umbilicus from my mother.

House of Puberty

When I was thirteen I went to live with my mother
and although we were in a doll's house estate
beside a slagheap in a Welsh mining village,
our living room was a jungle, my mother
on a sandbar. She'd sit in her rocking-chair
surrounded by caimans, begging me to save her.
Every evening, leafcutter ants marched off with her mind,
pieces of her thoughts dragged off in their jaws
to feed their fungus gardens. The carpet had towers
of termite nests which a giant anteater clawed open
and thrust his narrow snout into her cells.
He scooped up my mother's hopes with his endless tongue.
I had to keep clearing the mess, even when peccaries
filed in and threatened me with their tusks.
Parrots kept repeating that the Brazil nut of sanity
could only be gnawed open by an agouti.
Or a macaw! Maman would shout, and I'd have to agree,
though she also said scarlet macaws were her blood stains
streaking across our walls from my birth.
A tayra arrived once when she switched on the telly,
and curled up on her lap – the telly I watched as if
it would help us, its flickering leaf-light over our dark.
When The Forsyte Saga was on, and Soames
forced himself on his wife Irene, that's when
the harpy eagle crashed through our ceiling
and caught Maman's favourite monkey.
Our window was too large and through it
the neighbours watched, pointing and laughing.
She sat in her chair, rocking back and forth,
repeating, *I shouldn't have had children, shouldn't
have this trans-Amazon highway carved up my belly,
all these trucks bearing off with my virgin trees.*

I sat there as the logging trucks rumbled, and saw
tapirs crushed under their wheels. All I could do
was chant the names of roadkill – the boa who'd crept
so slowly trees grew on her, was the legendary Sachamama.
And a sky snake writhed on our floor like a rainbow
fallen to earth, its opal scales smashed.
Why did I do nothing? Why did I just sit there
wanting to be normal? The houses opposite looked
so ordinary, their children relaxed. They didn't have to watch
a rainforest burn in their living rooms, because
yes, as night fell, Maman would light her cigarette
and set the curtains alight, the curtains we didn't have.

Concert for Motherhood

(after Rebecca Horn)

If I say my mother was a piano I mean the grand
        in the children's home where I clung to one leg.

I'm old enough now to raise the lid and look at the strings
        and hammers inside, the harp of her nerves

as I try to recall tunes she played to me
        when I was in her body. If I say my mother was a piano

I mean the way the keys would turn into shark's teeth
        with one twist, and the grand would be hanging

from the ceiling upside-down, opening and closing
        its jaws trying to tell me something that must never

be set to music, something my cells remembered
        when they were brain-coral, my hands dead man's fingers.

Dumbo Octopus

She doesn't have an ink sac because
in her world there are no predators –
so deeply has she sunk. Imagine
the pressure, how many tons per inch.
That is her element and I'm
supposed to swim in it. Besides,
she's such a mistress of camouflage
she can vanish inside her own hide
instantly, and I'm left calling to her
through her door, asking what's wrong.
But she continues foraging for sea worms
and crustaceans as if I don't exist.
Her room sways with storms and tsunamis,
a ghost tape recorder plays swells of music
from when she sang in nightclubs –
a diva hugged by a salt-encrusted gown.
As soon as she was born she had to survive,
no mothering to speak of.
Males handed her sperm packets
and off she went laying her eggs,
crawling along the seafloor. And that's
how I arrived under the ocean's weight,
rolling it like Sisyphus through space.
No one has explored her realm and
no one will, but I remember it
from when I was just two inches high.
No one could keep her as a pet:
she would implode in a tank.
How I became human is another story,
how I can describe my mother to you
is the task I've spent my life attempting.
Every word I write bears the sea on it,
crushing my syllables under a thousand fathoms.

Monkey Muriel

There are monkeys in her head – night monkeys
that should be asleep during the day,
capuchins who are old people in child bodies,
they crack nuts and her mind breaks. Out
spill her thoughts to be eaten by sharp teeth.
The black spider monkeys are children covered
in pubic hair her husband has petted.
Here comes the procession of five-legged
babies with tails that grip her hand
and won't let go, pulling her through the trees.
The forest is full of frightened children –
sakis, uakaris, the woollies, titis, tamarins.
A pygmy marmoset huddles in her hair
and whispers *I am your daughter*,
then makes a nest in her chignon.
Her son is a red howler. He has a special sac
in his throat to make his voice carry for miles.
When he calls the humans listen.
Dr Pryce tries to describe the sound:
like a baby locked in his mother's womb
who grows teeth to bite his way out.
The patient sounds like a jungle of plucked parrots, he writes,
but his words loop across the page like lianas.
Muriel's howls make the hairs on his neck
stir like a bamboo thicket in a storm
and every cane draws blood as it whips
through the air of the battered forest.
All day the monkey-voices chatter, but
Dr Pryce has no answer, Muriel is speaking monkey.

My Book of the Dead

Those evenings when Maman tilted her face to the ceiling
and her eyes swarmed with visions, I crawled upstairs
to my room, soundproofed it by drawing a meadow
in the sketchbook called 'My Book of the Dead'.

I knelt by my Nile, among poppies and cornflowers
with blue Osiris butterflies. Oh, I knew my Egyptian gods
and how they could make someone die and come back
when it was safe, how they could scroll time

like a butterfly's proboscis, unroll it secretly
as sacred papyri. They taught me how to make
a night last three thousand years. My night-feeding
pollinator was not a moth but the butterfly nebula

which turned crayon dust to pollen on beaten gold
dunes. The landscape kept changing
as I tunnelled into ochre Ingres paper.
I was like Tutankhamun – my bedroom was a tomb.

I was not the undead in that underworld downstairs
where Maman reigned. By dawn, my drawing rippled
like a molten cornfield where I found myself
wrapped in bandages, locked in three nested coffins

guarded by the jackal Anubis. I taught myself to die,
only eighteen when I learnt to vanish. I dressed
in my finery for the afterlife, wore my scarab necklace
with its eyes of Horus, magic eyes of beetles.

I wreathed my face in olive leaves, poppies, cornflowers,
and as I adorned myself, I felt the hands of gods
flutter over me like butterflies, I saw the eyespots on
the underside of fingers. The tints of my cornflowers

did not fade through the long darkness,
my golds stayed un-plundered.
My two stillborn daughters in their mummies
uttered their first cries, next to a lock of my grandma's hair.

A fleet of model boats started to grow, like trees
that expand their girth beneath the bark, along
with wooden oars to row me to the field of rushes.
I was a girl-queen in my leopard-skin cloak

that Maman had forbidden me to wear, a sleep-
walker in the valley of queens, surrounding myself
with grave goods that showed I loved life. I hid
my voice in a silver trumpet shaped into petals

of a waterlily, engraved with hieroglyphs
that said: play me now if you want to be haunted.
Only my shadow rose from the dead,
only a sallow slip of a girl crept downstairs, her eyes

scrubbed of make-up, her cheeks scraped of poppy dye.
She braved what I could not – as my mother
lowered her gaze that had drilled through the ceiling
like a tomb robber into my inner chamber

to draw out of my sarcophagus a daughter who obeyed.

Photo of My Mother at Six Weeks

You're in a quilted basket,
in a christening gown
white as a snowy owl,
a gold locket around your neck
like an amulet. Perhaps it holds
the snow ghost's gold eye?
Behind you the net curtain
lifts in the draught
and the blue drape beside it
is embroidered with sun.
Your carrycot is shallow as the owl's nest –
just a scrape on the sill
where you've been lying for eighty years,
your tiny hands palm-up
out of organza cuffs
as if to clasp your mammy
who doesn't appear.
And as you doze,
the cottage around you crumbles.
You wake once in a children's asylum
where the calls of skuas
echo around the walls.
Then the dark years, pressed in an album
with pages airless as psychiatric wards,
and you with your sepia face
turned away from the light.

Maman

(after Louise Bourgeois)

If I say my mother was a spider,
I mean the giant ogress
who hangs at the dense
heart of my universe,

surrounded by her zodiac
of trussed stars. I mean
the great matriarch who
devours nighthawks and moons,

who with her eight stilettos
plucks an aeolian harp
whose space-time grid
is a sticky gold web

I blundered into just as
she was swaddling that
vine snake my father –
he who threshes in her silks.

Western Façade

Scaffolding shrouds the western façade, as my taxi
passes Notre-Dame. I have come to meet you again
after thirty-five years, Papa. Men clean the limestone
with brushes and lasers, millimetre by millimetre.
Each time I come, more is revealed, as if they
are working hard to make you clean, while you
lie on your sickbed, gasping for breath, your lungs
charred as the burnt rafters of a cathedral.
I have thought of you every day of my life, you say.
Your face, when you speak, shines like marble
through the scaffold of your oxygen mask.
Only after you die will I see your features clear,
as if centuries of grime have been scrubbed
from the colossus of your body, all history erased.

Skinner

Pass me my skin, Papa says – this is my cue to open
his wardrobe drawer and unfold the fur hide
with butterfly motifs he calls his *tigre mariposa*.

He used to lay it on the bed and ask me to lie on it,
my arms pinned out along the front paws, my legs
along the spreadeagled back paws.

Once upon a time, he begins, speaking in French –
il était une fois – jaguars could fly.
Then he shows me the bullet hole where

the heart once beat, and the thrumming starts.
Fetch me that cigar box he asks then, struggling
to breathe, and I obey. By the time

I reach him with the box I'm a child again.
I bring out the morpho butterfly inside, with eyespots
under its wings like jaguar eyes in the night

and I glide through a sky so blue-black Earth itself
is an eye. I don't know what happens while
I'm airborne, or where my father's trophy cat

takes me, but when I return there's always blood
under my nails and around my mouth,
my skin peeled off and folded in his drawer.

Hummer

I think of the unspoken, his airless room,
the words my father coaxed from his lungs
with the help of oxygen. The suitcase I found
on the shelf above his bed, with its jars
of mummified occupants, how I unwrapped
the photo curled around each hummingbird couple
like a sarcophagus, the smell of honey
mixed with formaldehyde, and how, when I prised
the male from the female, their throats
glowed like embers just above slit chests.
I saw it all then – a boy with his slingshot
in the forest at dawn, his hands pinning
the hummer's wings, the penknife slicing
through its narrow breast, its tiny heart torn out –
still beating, hot on my father's tongue.

The Lover's Bed
(after Rebecca Horn)

When my father tells me he treated himself
to an electric bed, I see morpho butterflies
tied to the bed frame by wires.
I see the sculptor Rebecca Horn
rigging mariposas with motors.
I see how their scales are crystals
that reflect tropical skies after death
and that my father still flies his familiars
through the cloud-forest night.

I see them flapping their ozone blue wings
to waft oxygen towards him. I press the switch
and they fly faster, until the room crackles
with summer lightning, each flash
the day he met my mother. The hotel room
where she worked as a maid swarmed with volts
as he flung her on the unmade bed
and tore off her blue uniform.
Her thighs opened like trembling wings,

her hymen a wingless butterfly
that Papa laughs at after ripping off
her wings. For the rest of her life
she'll be pinned to her bed, searching
for her innocence. For he just laughed
when someone opened the door
and he continued, all his doors opening
as if worked by pistons. Now the air quivers.
Now I see him, now I don't.

O aurora blue when I was conceived.
I make him sit up and down. I make his heart

flitter like a butterfly trapped in his chest,
I make his lungs turn zephyr blue,
his nights haunted by the startled eyes
of wing undersides. I flick him on and off.
I'm just a rotting banana on his jungle floor,
who he's drinking through the straw
of his proboscis, which is his oxygen tube.

O electric single bed for a lifelong bachelor.
O dead butterflies bluer than porn celluloid,
wearing motorised metal basques that
thrust your wings up and down, faster
and faster. O pitiless all-seeing eye of God.

Kisser

After you kiss me, my animals
swing above us, dangling from the bed canopy.

Are you frightened, Papa?
Let fire ants crawl down your ear canals!

Let hummingbirds coil their tongues around your brain
the way they wrap their tongues inside their skulls

after drinking nectar from a flower.
I've closed your eyes with thorns from the baby kapok,

plugged your nostrils and ears with beeswax –
how the bees stung me when I climbed to steal it.

When I told them what it was for, they helped me.
Only when the pale-winged trumpeters

forage on the moonlit floor
do I wake, screaming as I always do through closed lips,

my throat packed with soil
where you are buried.

I listen to the flock's tremolo, like wind through powerlines,
or your breath, Papa, as you come back to life,

climbing up the back of my throat,
gripping my baby teeth

to haul yourself once again out of my mouth.

The Insect Father

The moment I was born, you were a screw worm
feeding on my navel.

While I was a baby, you became a botfly
which bored through my fontanelle, lodged in my brain.

So when I learnt to talk, I named you:
Yellow Jack, Blue Devil, Black Vomit.

I watched you fly away from my childhood
to eat the face of God.

And when you visited me when I was eight
I saw your red eyes, red genitals,

bristles over your body like the pubic hair
I would one day sprout.

And when I had to pass to womanhood,
you were the mat of wasps

applied to my chest until my breasts grew.

To a Botfly

Because you're a botfly and I'm a trogon,
I've woven my nest near bad-tempered bees.

I've even allowed a cowbird cuckoo
to share my home, though it's a bully –

it'll gobble your grubs hatched in my skin.
And this is how it is in the canopy:

the bees protect me by attacking the flies,
but protect themselves by building their nest

inside a termites' nest, keeping anteaters from their hosts.
And so it goes on. A family of trogons

nests inside the bee nest inside the termite nest.
And this is why, when I'm arguing with you,

my little father, I wear a nest of masks.
When I've removed my termite face, my bee face,

cowbird and trogon faces, down
to the chattering chick that's hiding

beneath my skin, all I ask
is not to find a botfly father burrowing in my flesh.

The Pelts of Animals

Soon, the only wilderness
will be found in zoos,

carried on the coats of animals.

Swamps will dry out
into the scales of crocodiles

kept in a reptile house.
Rivers will be snakes in a vivarium.

Lions will wear our savannahs,
giraffes the shade of acacias.

The Siberian tiger
will be a walking birch forest,

on his breathing fur
branches will sway, not yet felled.

Cheetahs will circle like showers
after a long drought.

Too soon, the clouded leopard will sleep
in his lodge, snuggled in straw –

he will be our last tame storm, curled,
with his lightning-fangs closed.

The snow leopards
will mate in their hot cage

like two mountains
raising new Himalayas

with their colliding mantles,
their tails remnants of glaciers.

The gold jaguar will remind us
of the Amazon by day,

she bears its shadows
so briefly printed on her coat.

Her call to the black male
is day singing to night,

a creation myth in a lost language.
Here he comes, the galactic one –

on his pelt the zodiacs roam free.

Pale-winged Trumpeters

Three o'clock, it has stopped raining,
even the drips are quiet. A low purr

judders through the understorey
like a fleet of chicken-size starships

foraging the floor of outer space.
They sing from the depths of their bodies –

a long, descending *wuh-wuh-wuh-whir*
as they scratch for constellations

of fireflies, jewel-frogs, juicy planets
fallen from the trees of heaven –

this flock of black birds with white wings.
And when they find a termite's nest

they feast on the Milky Way,
while I listen to their electric tremolo

that might be a star swallowed,
as I am swallowed by the dark,

waiting for dawn's beak to open.

Vial

I sniff and sniff the rainforest in a vial
        the archivist hands out. I take a deep breath,

detect the understorey, that rank note of peccary,
        like a man who's been working down a mine

for weeks without washing, and I see again the herds that filed
        through the forest foraging for buried treasure. So deeply

am I drawn into the vial that I've forgotten the lookout male
        who once eyeballed me through fronds. His tusks are a

bass note that pierces my tongue. And then they all come back – the odours
        trees gave off to protect their trunks from predators:

the peccary tree, garlic tree, and even the ones we used to call shit trees.
        While others were built for flight, the walking palm with its mobile stilts

also has its essence here. I'm stumbling through vines, avoiding
        the young kapoks which wore armouries of spines

to defend themselves against agoutis and deer. And now I'm smelling
        the heart notes of the emergent layer, its flocks of parrots

with their fragrant wake of ozone and salts pecked
        from clay-lick caves they carved out with their beaks,

followed by a tang of the jaguar stalking the felt root-mat
        above their orange cliffs, a putrid caiman lingering on his breath.

I'm dizzy as the time I climbed the swaying steps
        of the canopy tower which shook with every gust,

so long ago the memory flickers, its top note of sunrise wavering.
        When I reached the platform and clung to the rail, I

could not look down or watch the monkeys gorging on fruit in crowns.
        Macaw pairs flew past me, their wingtips brushed my head,

their tails streaming out in pungent blues and reds, a taste in my mouth
        like rust plumes down a drain. Then I look further out

over emerald tides of leaves to the quicksilver river and
        the purple mountains beyond, their blessing of far-off rain just

a trace of smoke at the bottom of the vial, mixed with mercury vapour
        which I must not inhale, before I replace the stopper.

II

The Camargue and Languedoc

On Longing

If you could talk, you'd tell me about nightingales
singing loudest at night, you'd explain that only
the males sing, to lure females from the skies
as they arrive from their migrations.
Like drawing down the stars? I'd ask, then
we'd list the galaxies flying through your night.
You'd know everything about flight,
even the starling nested in the catalpa tree
outside your bedroom window once:
how urgently the parents flew to and fro
to feed their chicks inside the nest-hole
and how the father perched on a branch
when they fledged, as if smoking a well-earned cigar.
You'd know every bird in the reedbeds –
the chuckles and creaks of the great reed warbler,
the piercing notes of Cetti's warbler,
and the one that wears a moustache like you.
You'd rave about the roller – his celestial
wings and sienna back. There'd be so much
time for us, so much time,
I would float on clouds of your breath,
somersault through smoke-rings
clean as morning steam from the swamp, to see
nightingale eggs olive green as new worlds.
To hear you describe again how sheer
the male's bill becomes when open
in sunlight, notes tumbling up in torrents of desire.
I go back to the Camargue and listen
for you speaking through birds. I roost in your tree
just outside your window, my mouth open, waiting
for your words to be dropped in – grasshoppers,
cicadas, beetles. I even long for the worms
tunnelling that fertile cosmos you're buried in.

My father, perched outside our nest,
smoking a Gitane. My wandering father, camped
on the shore of Saintes-Maries-de-la-Mer,
always on the move, paused now, proud
of your task done, raising a daughter strong
enough to grow wings, to peer at Earth from her
migration, where a voice calls her to come home.

The Lammergeier Daughter

That night, I opened your wardrobe and found
a trophy of vultures, their necks pierced

by hanger hooks. I saw at once
that you hunted everything I loved –

the griffon, the Himalayan, the lammergeier,
who haunted our home with wheeling cries.

I peeled off my skin then, and robed myself
as a bird bride. Veiled in morning mist

I married the sky. Of course, you aimed
at my heart, but as the bullet tore through me

I wrapped my talons around your skull,
lifted you high, and dropped you as a lamb

drops newborn from his mother
onto the snow-fleeced earth.

I landed beside you on the quilt.
And when the flesh-eaters had done their work,

it was I, your lammergeier daughter,
who devoured your bones – look, Father,

how they slide down my throat like rifles.

Civet de Cerf

We are eating braised buck, while Papa
talks about hunting with his papi,

the rifles that were tall as him,
the twelve points on one stag, how it

reared into the sky. The hair on my head
stood upright, he says, like antlers.

And as he speaks, he opens the cabinet
where he keeps his antique guns:

a Versailles hunting rifle embossed
with gold, silver and platinum,

a flintlock shotgun in its red silk case,
as if I'd rummaged inside his chest

and retrieved his heart.

Papa Guêpier

Only after you die do I dare open that case I always gazed at
when the minutes stung.

It emitted a low hum as if to comfort me. Only now
do I find it full of bees. I don't know how they survived.

I tell them our predator is gone as they crawl out
and climb up my arms to mass on my face.

I can smell meadows of nectar, the honey
they made from wildflowers on Mont Aigoual.

I want you to taste your beloved Cévennes. Now I'm the girl
in a bee mask, I let my swarm of wings shimmer

in waves over my cheeks to mesmerise your ghost.
I am the bee queen now, my workers are this mask

I must wear to face Papa the bee-eater, you
who sit opposite me every day, your beak poised to feed.

Choker

(a haibun for the Bête du Gévaudan)

I go down the steps to the basement, into the morgue where they are preparing you. I use waterproof inks, draw the downy under-fur before embedding the roots of wolf-hairs in your skin. If I plant enough you will warm under my fingertips and your chest will rise and fall with the wolf heart inside, the beast that lives as long as my needle works.

I drop one rose on your coffin. And when the soil has covered you, and the gravediggers have left, I dig like a bitch after a bone she has buried long ago. I have been digging all my life, searching for my father.

Just as a dog must wear a spiked collar to hunt a wolf, so I wear my choker of thorns to visit your grave. I wear it inside out, so the spikes stab my neck as your teeth did once – I am your dog rose.

O father whom I have lived inside like an undigested Red Riding Hood, my body pierced by the briary of your blood. I have tattooed under-hairs all down your legs, yes, even in that place dark as a cave where a fire ignites, and out of the sparks flies a ravenous pack. I stippled them sleeping in your lap, my red wolf-flowers, whose snouts are bound with thorns.

I lie on your plot as you once lay on me. My face opens like a wild rose that has stayed muzzled too long. It is time for it to open, petal by petal, until the flower of my lips starts to speak:

Let me rest now on
your thigh, quiet as a pup who's
fed on mama's milk.

After visiting the Museum of Doors, Pézenas,

I crept down the spiral steps onto the earth
floor of my own museum of doors –
warped portals down each side of me

led to caves of electric and gas meters.
Each door was marked with the numbers
of the beast inside mathematics.

I was six, learning to count to a hundred.
Below me, Papa warned, raged a fire
where wolves would leap from flames.

Shall I call those wolves bêtes du Gévaudan?
Or shall I call them to me like a shepherdess,
stroke their long muzzles and scythe claws

that mark them as loups-garous, hyena-
mastiffs, chimeras of my nights?
Shall I train them to turn on Papa when

his face peers through the wavy window
at the top of the stairs and his double enters?
Some meter doors open onto vistas of Lozère,

its granite mountains and ravines,
while in others Papa is playing hide and seek,
tick-tock go the meters like his heartbeat.

In one cupboard the birds he shot
re-hatch from their corpses and fly to help me.
Papa's face is covered with a cloth

and there are two of him and two of me.
Other-me hovers just below the ceiling
that bulges with cables like his veins –

she's watching what he does to his daughter.
Then she glides through the sky's warp drives
where every star is a keyhole

for angels to watch and remember.
I open my doors which are trees in the wolf-wood
where a little girl plays with her doll

dressed as a boy, clothing her little father
in a wolf-mask and fur pyjamas that she keeps
taking off and putting back on. She strips him

to the bones she's drawn on his body,
and, around the bones, in permanent ink,
a museum of doll doors that she keeps knocking on

with the hand-shaped knocker of her adult hand.

The Frozen Zoo

> You must collect things for reasons you don't yet understand
> DANIEL BOORSTIN

Go to the cellar of your childhood and stay when the light switch
   clicks off. Find your father's mini-fridge, the one he kept beside the bed
      he died in, his last birthday gift to himself, next to the crates

of vintage champagne bought for your reunion. His pet fridge
   that he pleaded with, on winter mornings when he could hardly breathe.
      It has the blue light of rime, racks of miniature glass towers.

Here are the vials he saved for you, smoking in the dark, as if
   savouring his last cigarette above the steps
      he could no longer descend, hooked as he was to oxygen.

Your father, perhaps the last human on earth, so precious
   when you first met him again after thirty-five years. Open
      the long-closed stoppers. You know what to do.

The voices that have been telling you to collect and collect will sigh
   as you get to work. They are all here – Sudan the last white rhino,
      Benjamin the thylacine, and Saaya the black leopard,

spirit of the Kabini forests, his stem cells with their tuft of fur.
   For reasons you don't yet understand, you must imagine them
      alive, strong enough to bear your weight on their backs.

Now, mount their ghosts and go back in time, your hands around
   the neck of years, and ride down the long tunnels of the cellar
      where memories are stored. Some will be too painful,

but you'll fly through them, reach your father just before he dies.
   Whatever he has done is done, the champagne takes you both
      down strata, past rows of meter cupboards, the one

with a child's mattress and the doll whose lips you sewed shut
    so she wouldn't tell. Down the catacombs you must go, through
        the crypts and wells of the under-cities built one over another.

Here is the room where your animals sleep. Now imagine them back into being,
    imagine the old forests, trees that took eras learning to transform
        toxic air to oxygen will sprout up as you arrive. Find the test tube

where your own cells are preserved in liquid nitrogen, for this
    is how you become a child again. No man has forced himself into you,
        no doctor has to come after the one you trusted turned you inside out.

You'll find glaciers of tears and blood. As they thaw,
    they'll turn into raging brown rivers to replenish the earth.
        Now open each vial and release the captives from your frozen zoo.

Bac du Sauvage

Not the ferry itself across the Petit Rhône
nor the narrow road between the river
and the canal through marsh leading to it,

not the low powerlines like bunting
along one side, with songbirds silhouetted
against the sun on this savage land.

Not even when, if we stared at them long enough,
their colours would reveal them to be
bee-eaters scanning the sky for insects.

Not how, when we reached the barge, we turned
back to be on the right side of the road,
closer to them, as if we could catch our lives

in our mouths as easily as they snatched
wasps in their flight. As if we could stop
the car and snap them up with our camera,

take their quintessence home, then peer
at the shots for glints of us in their red eyes.
No, not even how beautiful we could be

in chestnut, gold and turquoise raiment
reflecting tints of the atlas
as we migrate across the hungry globe –

what if we could rub all the world's harms
from the air as they do, dash hornets' tails
against the post, until their stings break off?

Ode to Causse Méjean with Takhi Horses
(for my 70th birthday)

A day so happy I vault the electric fence   am with the Takhi horses
whose name means spirit   I bear the bites to my neck

the flies that mob muscles   the open wounds
along my flanks are badges that say   look how I tried to live

like a foal that's never been harnessed   see how I wear their zigzags
on my knees   and how some days   I'm a maze of hairpin bends

that spiral the gorges surrounding this plateau   how I'm gouged
by the rivers Tarn and Jonte   today my mind is a rapture

of vultures soaring over the cliffs   look how I race over Causse Méjean
as if it too is a wild stallion   its thistles my stiff mane

how even Aven Armand   that cathedral cave bristling with stalactites
beneath the pelt of this Causse   is my chasm

how constellations of ammonite seas   layer my skin
that each pore on my seventy-year-old face   is a porthole

to fairy caverns   anyone who abseils down them emerges
as if from a dream   their skull stuccoed with grottoes

that each blemish is a rock in the Chaos de Nîmes-le-Vieux
that the breath playing stone organ-pipes is mine   that the endless

night where time drips is my drawn-out bliss   O limestone moor
where each grey hair bursts into sun-flare   this birthday when my feet

cleave into hooves and the clouds of dust I trample   and will return to
are seedbeds of new stars   head high as the Horsehead Nebula

Chemin des Rainettes

What do nightingales eat?
They darted onto the path
before us again and again,

a green bug in their beaks.
Caterpillars? Shield bugs?
Crickets? Or earth's music?

What alchemy turns a cockroach
into starlight, a fly into a song
that tears night's veil?

Tiny frogs plop
into the ditch as we approach
the beginning of a score.

But the nightingales are no longer audible
as we try to remember
their notes, because to progress

along the Chemin des Rainettes
means having to walk in tune.
The sun is too hot, the mistral

blows cold, the tamarisk bushes
hold us tenderly, see how
our shadows are still brushed

by their feathery flowers
and the hooks of bramble blossoms
trail cells of our skin like pollen.

Look! the nightingales are silhouetted
against the burning disc, plucking
music from the flutes of our bones.

The Beast of Vaccarès

Only once did my father speak at length, his room
darkening as he described the beast – half man
half goat, huge, with horns and hooves.
A weak and old demigod, dying like me,
he said, raising his hand as if it held a flute
only he could play, until every buckthorn
and mastic thicket bent to hear his notes.
On sandbars of the lagoon wolves and lynxes gathered.
There was a full moon, Papa said, and I rode
my horse Clair de Lune, he bucked then shivered.
I stood still as a juniper, every needle-
leaf on my neck strained to listen.
I've told you about the songs of the swamps,
with samphire alight everywhere, swaying to the mistral.
I've told you about the sea horses galloping
on the shore, white as ghosts? Now see
this other ocean – black, horned, and dancing
around the goat-man, bulls trampled and gored
in their crush to worship him, herds
bellowing to his music, more and more
arriving from every field, to circle the demon,
a whirlpool of snorting bulls, as many as waves in the sea.
Then they turned and raced counter-clockwise,
their hides glinting with starlight.
And then what? I asked. Ah, that old beast
who roamed the tangled islets of Vaccarès
was swallowed by the Bull-drowner – that pit
of quicksand. Then my father became quiet,
and never again spoke about the Beast of Vaccarès,
or his beloved Camargue where flamingos flock
like symphonies of blood, or the hoof-drums
of wild black bulls with harps for horns.
But I'd seen the moonlight in his black eyes

and how he breathed easily for once, breath
that now sank into the quagmire of his lungs.
I sat opposite him every mealtime, hoping
for another tale, for there are many monsters
in that delta, and after every dessert, I peered
into the abysses of his black eyes
but all I glimpsed was my own face drowning.

Courses Camarguaises

What if you didn't go to the bullrings in Spain,
but instead watched the gentler games
of the Camargue where black bulls are the stars?
It's their names that top the bill, not matadors.

What if you sat in the front row when Goya
chased the raseteur over the barrier and
charged at the crowd, before trampling
his victim, so that ambulances came rushing.

What if you thought that sticking banderillas
in a bull's shoulders before plunging a blade
into his neck, is cruel? If you knew that even the beasts
who win those games are killed off-stage afterwards.

I see you now, my father, proud of these marshes
where bulls roam free, retired young enough
to enjoy half a lifetime in peace, before being buried
upright with their heads turned to the sea,

a statue erected in the square in their honour.
Can you hear their lyre horns playing
deep underground? The song of masculine power
harnessed for a time, then released through

every grass blade, saltpan and tamarisk leaf,
to surge in the soft waters of the Rhône delta
which is itself a lyre, insisting that tenderness
is here on earth – just beneath our feet.

The Tarasque Tattoo

The mortician turned my father on his front
and there she was, drawn on his back, so lifelike
she seemed to be growling:

Lagadigadèu, let me out, I'm going to dance!

I looked at his demon, heard
the song Papa always chanted
as he stole into my room.

I faced the chimera with the fangs of a lion,
her body shielded by a spiny carapace.
She had six bear paws, as if it was she

who had run up and down his spine
as he pounced, while, coiled over his tail,
her dragon tail thumped the beat of the wild,

telling him to pierce me with his scorpion sting.
I knew that the monster my father hid
was me, that the child in the Tarasque's jaw

was also me, impaled and helpless.
I knew that the ink scratched in his blood
was his hated mother, 'who made me do bad things,'

he'd said, 'who sent me to the Jesuit school.
You don't know what the priests did to me!'
I thought of the hybrid etched on his skin

like a painting of an extinct lion in a cave,
how one pure girl had tamed the Tarasque.
And I wondered why the mob had to hurl rocks

at the beast when she'd been tamed,
led like a lamb on a leash by Saint Martha
after she'd sprinkled holy water over its horns.

All it took was her sash, and the world
was safe from its scourge.
Could I have tamed my Papa? Led on the leash

of an oxygen tube, following me down
the paths of his room where he would die –
Lagadigadèu, let me out, he says, *I'm going to dance!*

Camargue Bull at Dusk

The swamp pounds with frog song – a loud throb
that pulls me outside towards the black oaks, soundwaves
so high they must breach human hearing.
Surely the stars are singing in their spiral loops,

day mating with night. I've come to see the wild
herd in their favourite copse, far off, just a blur
of black humps, but their crescent horns
catch rays of sunset and moonrise.

I want to see one up close, and who knows what
could happen, summoned by the bullfrogs,
a Mithraic chant to lure a bull. And the spell works,
because their leader comes bounding

to the gate I'm leaning on. I back away,
nervous of these stars of the arena, their
crowd-charging bucks. But his off-key bell
clangs a welcome and I touch the broad black nose

he offers me just as a small white butterfly
lands on it then flies away. The frogs increase
their volume, and now I hear castanets
of throat-sacs pump with joy at being here,

even if just for one microsecond – to be alive
at the threshold, this orchestra
of stellar instruments echoing across the delta.
The bull thrusts his opal horns through the gate,

asking me to join him and every living pulse.
And now I'm so awake I shiver in the heat,
my flimsy nightdress no shield against what
happens next: the lyre of his horns I must stroke

as if to play his music, whatever danger it might
bring, his hulk caged behind the staves, his head
haloed with flies and mosquitoes – quavers
and semiquavers flitting through the air to bite me.

Hide (Emperors and Egrets)
(poem beginning with a line by John Burnside)

Give me a childhood again and I will live
with a father who shows me
dragonflies coupling on the wing
and a mother who points to the little egret
where the emperors have swooped
too low in their ecstasy and are in his beak.
Give me a mother who teaches me to look
through binoculars at the egret's eye
as he gulps the female and the male escapes.
Give me parents who reveal the harsh world
but insist it's beautiful. Who let me uncrumple
my transparent wings for the sun to light up
as if my body is a stained-glass chapel
no parent must smash as I learn to fly.
Oh, I would watch everything with my
compound eyes, see how in some light
my mother's hair has solar flares, and
when my father frowns, prisms
dance on his glasses. Give me a childhood
again, and I promise to read the swamp
like a holy book with words hungry
as mosquitoes, singing rhapsodic hymns
around my face, and when they bite,
to keep looking through the narrow vent,
waiting in the gloom for the next revelation.
And I'll keep waiting, because, just as my spirit
slips through the planks into the mire,
a spoonbill lands like an archangel
no parent could have prepared me for
even if they'd told me bedtime stories, while
I cowered in the blind of my bed.
Give me a childhood again and I will find

the courage to hear the tale of the assassin
bug which stung a baby just as she was born.
Even from the hide of my infancy,
my eyes will grow new cells
and I will catch my life like this great
egret which flies up from the marsh,
a huge snake dangling from her claws.

Ode to the Camargue

> Wet as a water lily,
> the flamingo opened the doors
> of its rosy cathedral,
> and flew like the dawn
>
> PABLO NERUDA

Your waterlilies are wings of rosy flamingos opening their dawns.
You are imparadised with mornings of wild blue iris skies.

And just as the lower petal of an iris reflects the upper,
so your rice swamps are sky flowers with rays for anthers.

Your reeds harbour tussock moth caterpillars and vagrant darters
with red-gold abdomens and wings where sunrays are harp-veined.

Your goatsbeard clocks have strong taproots, giant globes
dispersed by winds, your hours are seedhead slow.

O oriole- and roller-miraged, kingfisher-streaked
bee-eater shivered air,

la Vièro ié Danso, Old Dancer, maker of mirages,
show me your ditches harbouring viperines and crayfish,
your carpenter-bee'd thistles clustered with snails,

your knapweed canal verges. Lead me between crown-vetch
and toadflax while Nala the Dutch shepherd dog dives

into every pool then rolls in dust! Let her be my guide on strolls
in the realm of the conehead mantis!

O sansouires of samphire and sea lavender
between the lou petit and lou grand Rose!
Rhône delta where saltworks dredge Earth's tears of laughter.

O Camargue mares! You rise from your marshes in a herd of galloping days
with ebony and silver foals cradled inside, days within days!

You birth the Bioù – prize black bulls of nights horned with crescent moons.
Your wheat fields are gold-strung harpsichords played by kestrels.

Every dwarf oak is blessed with nightingales,
every tree has as many harmonies as leaves!

Your skies are herds of mistrals and tramontanes trampling
silver-backed leaves of poplars and pines,

your skies echo with the clacking beaks of white storks
bringing frogs and lizards to nestlings,
their wingbeats like the swish of heavenly gates.

Your heart is the lagoon of Vaccarès, shirred mirror where flamingos nest.
O mud nests where dawns hatch from eggs!

Hide (Mosquitoes)

When my father appears
        dressed in a suit of mosquitoes,

their high-pitched whine like a siren –
        I want to save him

before he vanishes
        again. I'm visiting him in his hide.

I spend hours with my binoculars,
        looking out through

the narrow vent, at the view
        he remembers – the night

heron and purple heron, the spoonbill,
        and the one bittern that's been

booming through all his internment,
        beyond the chug of the machine

that pumps oxygen into his nostrils,
        whose sound I think is my heart.

Only as I leave do I notice
        my wasp spider mother

cleaning her palps at the centre of her orb
        above the exit.

Her survival depends
        on trapping all his mosquitoes

and when she finishes
        once again I won't have a father,

because his suit of singing blood is all
        there is left of my childhood.

Hide (My Birth)

I go into the hide, a finger hushes me
        as I enter the dark with its slit
                of swamp light, a blindfold in reverse.

SILENCE ABSOLU, the notice says.
        Do they sense me, those waders
                in dawn's brackish waters?

A breeze drifts through like a breath
        though I have no mouth yet,
                all that is human just a bird-mother.

My mother smells of wood but I have no
        nose, yet every nerve in my body-to-be
                waits for a rip of paradise blue,

for the one whose quills are forged
        by angels, whose beak is a knife.

Letter to Muriel

Let me try again, dear Maman, now I know
your name means archangel Muriel
in the dominion sphere of heavenly hosts.

Above you only the six-winged seraphim
and the four-winged and faced cherubim
with their ox, eagle, lion, and human masks,

their bull hooves polished like burning brass,
and the Thrones, fire wheels revolving with eyes.
Let me try again to see the angel that pierced

your small unglazed bedroom window,
who only showed you one wing
but that was too much, you dived under your sheet

and just the tip brushed your forehead.
One icy plume turned your brain to crystal
and there followed mute and nameless

months in the blank ward. I'm trying
to imagine your face with no eyes or mouth.
I've had to paint them in, year by year

as I aged and you've almost become normal,
at least in my portraits. I see you now,
describing each pearl feather, each a different

colour you've never seen since. Your face
still shines with blinding light, even as
the ambulance takes you to a children's asylum

when you are only nine. I'm almost with you
years later, when we're in our vineyard and you
press your finger to your lips, order me to listen

because your angel is singing. I hear its silver notes,
a high-pitched trill that pulses in and out
as if its voice is shuddering as it enters our air.

And then we see it perched on the fig tree
like an insect, the jade-white body
and translucent wings with veins that are

your map home. It's just a snowy tree cricket
I tell you, but you say it's the angel Muriel,
which is how you have dominion over me because

it means you are saintly and must be obeyed,
that if I am good you will love me.
I can see the stars, and the parts of the sky

without stars, where the Grézac and Larzac plateaux rear.
I listen to the song of carboniferous night,
before any bird appeared on the earth, the song

that must have been beyond dinosaur hearing
and aren't we dinosaurs to the angels? Aren't we
stone buried in rock that they have to crack to get to us?

Your face has the lit-up look it got at Mass
after communion. The song slower and sadder
in the cooling nights at the end of our summer.

Even though I know it is only an insect
I try mixing the colours that fuse in white,
the ones you said appeared in the woodland cottage.

At times, the rising heat turns my sketch
quicksilver. But I'm hacking through ice
to get to you, your face that I draw on Ingres paper

is buried in the glacier of years. You've just given birth
to me, and to lower your fever the nurses have packed you
in ice, while I'm carried away to a glass box.

Two weeks I struggle to live, before I'm whisked
to another country to live with your mother.
It is snowing. Someone is plucking live archangels

in heaven's garden, relentlessly as a factory machine
plucks chickens until all that's left is the naked
pockmarked flesh to be deep frozen.

Which is what it feels like when my first boyfriend
explains there are no angels, just hallucinations.
I must have entered that word with its mirrored halls,

its nations of light like truth serum.
What I want to tell you is that I believe. I think
Angel Falls is a god moving through our dimension,

flakes of its feathers pummelled by cliff gusts,
the smoke that drops for almost one mile
pierces the earthbound like buckshot,

that probably this is just one of its wings
and that more would kill, though even one was enough
to drive you mad. Perhaps angels can only be seen

if they're shrunk to the scale of an insect. Listening
to the tree cricket's song, with its churr
like a white flame guttering, tells me what

you must have heard when you were a child
in your bed, each pearl a note beyond hearing.
Was that when you became cool to the touch,

Muriel whom I could never hug?
They locked you in a padded cell, like a cricket
in a matchbox. They plunged you in hot and cold baths

and electrocuted your temples until
all you could feel was needle-sharp spray
of the mile-high wing, then the plunge pool

where your childhood drowned. Above you,
the wheels covered in eyes revolved
as you became the perfume of God, which is how myrrh

morphs into the name Muriel at God's Throne,
around which the seraphim fly, crying holy holy holy.
Their hooves are heavy as brass and kick like bulls

and all there is between you and heaven
is a glassine veil. I'm trying to love you now, mother
who was always packed in frost tissue paper,

a gift I must never open.

The Walnut Tree

When my brain was small as a walnut
the horses came.
They cantered in in their fireproof shoes,

their eyes glowing like keyholes
of my mother's womb.

After my birth, the unripe nut of my mind
had a milky flavour Maman liked to bite into –
I could not stand up to her.

But when I reached puberty
I mounted my stallion,

the one whose muscles gleam like wood,
whose mane is a forest fire.

He carries me into our vineyard
and finds the walnut tree at the centre,

as once I slipped into my mother's body.
And I pray to the gods of the walnut groves:

I have tied a lock of my mother's hair
from your leaves like a spark.
I have brought my stone doll

from the stone age of my childhood
and laid it at your roots.
I have tied my favourite stallion to your trunk.

Some nights, he only stands by my side and quivers.
Some nights, Maman makes me break
his backbone with one of your branches.

Maman Argiope

When I looked up from pushing through brambles
    I was eye-level with a wasp-spider,
tigress of the sous-bois, gold and black orb-weaver,
        zipper or writing spider. She was oscillating
the white zigzag at the centre of her web. I did
    what any hornet would do and backed away from the tapestry
on which she'd embroidered honeybees and pasha butterflies
       in silk trusses, a lizard swaddled in the corner.

I knew this wasn't one of my aura migraines
    but she was making auroras vibrate from her stabilimentum,
writing glyphs with her spinnerets that meant no entry
       beyond here, no trespassing into the underwood
nature has reclaimed from your vineyard.
    That drystone hut you once camped in, she said,
with its spring and barrel where a viper drank,
       are scrawled in my lightning forks, the chair

you leapt onto when rats dropped on your face at night,
    is gone, is gone, as is the ant-proof cupboard where you kept sugar.
Your beaten floor is no longer beaten.
       Your camp-bed sleeps, half buried in the wall.
You won't find traces of humans beyond me, she sang,
    though her singing was more like a susurration
from our terraces buried under sessile oaks.
       The threads that barred my way were strings

of a thorny rain-harp on which woodchat shrikes
    had impaled a gallery of scarabs, a firecrest.
My arms and legs were scratched with labyrinths
       but I could not tell if the ink was blackberry or blood.
I told the orb-weaver that my mother once lived with me here,
    before the vines were uprooted and sold. I confessed

that my mother was almost happy then and I was only
>	a little frightened of the one who's gone, and has left me

a vineyard with no grapes in, who's plucked their roots from my eyes.
>   My job had been to scream *au secours!* if Monsieur Gali

came to the door at night, from his ruin deep in the woods
>	where he lived on game caught with his gun.

Are you writing this down, Maman Argiope? I asked.
>   Or did I dream it all? Did it pass across my retina and every time

I get a migraine I see you guarding your
>	vineyard of rods and cones in the lens of my eye.

Hide (Red Crayfish Claws and a Glossy Ibis)

I want to believe that the red crayfish claws
on the planks above the water
are not my mother's stilettos
thrown on the hotel floor by my father
in his impatience to ravish her,

that the hulking grey herons inside the hide,
caught by the camera trap at night,
are not her hallucinations hunting her.
Night after night, she made me sit
on the side of her bed while she told me

about men – how they gobble girls up
like herons with their spear beaks.
I don't want to believe this, because
if men are bad then all there is
in the world is her. The swamp

is salted with tears, my eyes
swollen to slits as I peer out
from the hide of my face – a plain
hut from which, for the rest of my life
I'll gaze out for one glimpse

of a glossy ibis. I don't mind that he'll
devour me, I just want to see his bridal plumage
shot with honeymoons and sunbeams –
that one time I went to a nightclub
and danced with him in the strobe light.

My Mother's Provençal Dress

When I was eighteen I stole my mother's
Provençal dress while she was in hospital,
and walked into the art school canteen
wearing the wood that grew over our vineyard –
the overgrown paradise she had bought so we
could be together every summer holiday.
Interlaced branches of kermes and pubescent oaks,
how I love your moss and grape gathers,
your stitching like a hidden brook,
the shoulder straps like garden bridges
over to the reeds and rushes patch.
You could almost hear the cicada thrum
threaded round my waist. The quilted brocade
panels over my breasts and around the full hem
splashed sunlight over me as I entered
the studio in a Librium haze. Cornflowers
and poppies, Adonis blue butterflies,
blessed my body as I stood in the corridor
and my mood rose and fell like the lift.
And when evening came, the tree crickets began
their whispers from the fig tree. If I tell you
the hottest third year painter asked me out,
you might forgive me that I didn't return her dress,
after that first date when I stayed out too late
and was punished. I wore it every day until
it began to tear. I invisibly-mended each leaf,
my needle was an adder flashing in and out
of the undergrowth. Even then, when Maman
had come home, I hid her dress in the secret
pocket of my bag, under pills and forbidden makeup,
and changed in the Cardiff station toilets
on my way to college, and took it off on my way
back, along with my mascara and dog rose lipstick.

I sat as I was told on the edge of Maman's bed
and said I was evil over and over until she was
satisfied and let me leave. She didn't know I was a thief
though she accused me but had no proof.
At night I'd listen to the vines drinking oxygen,
turning water to wine, and I'd call the shy
ocellated lizard who has sky blue eyes
along his flanks that witness everything –
I coaxed him from his rock to watch over me.

III

Tala Zone

(Madhya Pradesh, India, and Paris)

Tala Zone

1

Father, I have made the iron gate to our building spring open, I have slipped through the inner glass door. I have rung the caretaker's bell and explained why I need to see the cellar and he has let me in. It's as if I've climbed over the gate of Tala Zone before dawn and entered the tiger reserve alone, no jeep to protect me. The spotted deer stand watching, their breath rising in the predawn light, their ears pricked for the slightest twig crack, betraying the arrival of predator.

The track is sandy, glows in the moonlight. I bend down, can see fresh pugmarks, large and round: a male. I am going the right way. The forest guard is asleep in his hut. It is here that the ground slopes down, like these spiral steps. I look up, surprised to see a window at the top of the cellar. I've always dreamt there was a window. I am inside my dream.

But this time, you are alive, Father, able to breathe, thanks to the oxygen machine pumping in a corner of your room. Alive enough for me to have asked you for the number of our building in the Boulevard de Grenelle, where we lived together when I was a child. Even when I travel as far as India, you are with me and I am re-entering our cellar.

Take a deep breath, do that pursed lip breathing you must do. Watch your heart doesn't race. The pump is exhaling, inhaling and I am walking, walking. No one is allowed inside the core of Bandhavgarh National Park after sunset. No one is allowed inside this cellar at the bottom of our building. But the caretaker has heard my story and unlocked the door. He told me not to stay long because there are rats down here and a bad smell from the poison.

I press the light switch at the top of the stairs and the moon comes out from behind a tree. Round and round I go, right down to the bottom, to the earth floor. I must not wake the monkeys: they must not bark a warning. Here is the smell. I recognise it as male tiger spray, and the stench of the remains of a carcass, just behind the lantana bushes. A rat snake slithers past on the path in front of me.

Why is the cellar forked, Father? Why does it grow narrower? My path is flanked by thorny bamboo, by evergreen sal trees. Why is everything coated in dust? How small must I become, to pass under the roof that bulges with electric cables like banyan vines? How do I know which are live? And why do the sal trees and the crocodile bark trees and the dhok trees look like rough doors that I must open? I don't remember these doors from my recurring dream. I don't remember this ticking, like a hundred clocks behind each door labelled with a numbered plaque. I think of other cellars, how going to the toilet in a restaurant always means going downstairs, deep into the musty Parisian underworld with its honeycomb of limestone crypts and shallow drains.

I'm in the cellar's forest and the moon is shining. Between me and the moon there's a man with a cloth over his face. Is it you, Father? I never thought it was you when I was six, but I'm grown-up now. It must be you, because who else would have sent me to the cellar, told me to count to a hundred but not to go down to the very end because a fire was there with tigers leaping out?

I open the door to the first electricity meter and you are there, Father, your fists held out, asking me to guess which one. I point to the left and you open it, saying 'Look! Precious gold.' But what I see is an amber eyeball. Then you close your fist again and I can't see you, or where the way back out is, everything is dark, and the moon has dipped behind the trees. Then I realise you're holding the eye of a newborn tiger cub. That its other eye is in your other hand.

You are sitting on a child's mattress, and you're asking me to face you, so you can stitch up my eyelids and lips with bamboo thorns. You say I mustn't cry. I should remember that the caretaker is upstairs, that the forest guard will hear me if I scream. But I don't. There is only the cellar with a forest inside and a series of rough doors that I must open. I can still see through the thorns but everything is red and blurred. My nightdress is pulled up around my neck so I tug it down. I can't open my mouth to scream, so the sound I make is strangled, as if I'm still asleep.

From now on I won't speak to anyone. I will be a mute daughter, just like a newborn cub, or make only muffled squeaks.

I open the second door and find myself in a hide, high up in a mahua tree. I sit watching the Malabar pied hornbill bring figs to his mate. The female has walled herself up in a nest hole in the tree opposite, cemented herself in with a fruit paste, so no snake can eat her eggs. There's a rush of air when the male lands with his huge wingbeats. I watch as he regurgitates his meal and pipes it through the great curved bill with its black-and-yellow casque down into the tip of hers through the slit of her cell. He arrives every hour and each time he feeds her I feel stronger.

I retrace my steps to where the cellar forks. Now I must go down the right fork. The roof is lower as if only made for children. Here too there are doors rough as tree bark and so many electric cables it's like walking under the tails of langurs and leopards in a grandmother banyan. You are calling me, Father, from behind the first door. It opens and you show me your good-luck charm that you've carried since childhood, a leopard's paw. Now the deer watching me from the end of the tunnel have multi-branched antlers, a ghost forest in the dusty predawn light and as I descend they get bigger, towering above me like forest gods. An elephant calf presses himself against me, cuddling me with his trunk. His eyes are brandy topazes. He too is a god.

The next door opens to a night black as bear fur, its muzzle bleeding after eating honey baited with explosives. I want to ask you how my teddy-bear mama's face exploded, Father. Who would plant gunpowder inside honey? But you're telling me to dance. You push a thin cane through my nose and sing and huff, sing and puff, while you jerk the cane, teaching your bear cub the steps. I have to remind myself that it is I who have brought the wonders of my grandmother's jungles into the cellar. My Indian grandmother, who took care of me when I was a baby, whom I will return to soon. As I think of her, I start to dance backwards, out of the meter cupboard and down to the very end of the cellar.

I open the last door on the left of the right fork and there's a peacock inside. I can hear Maman saying how vain you were, how you slept in, then spent every afternoon doing your toilette, before going out to your nightclubs. I've been into the jazz cellar in the rue de la Huchette, next door to the Hôtel Les Argonautes where you lived. But this peacock has a girl's face. She is dressed in a wedding gown with a train made of peacock feathers and no one is here to give her away, there's not even a groom. Her dress is sapphire-emerald as the Earth from space, and her train is erect, rustling like wind through dry grass. Her train surrounds her head in a halo of eyes, all watching me, like atolls in the Indian ocean held up on waves of plumes. The stars have offered me their eyes, to bear witness. They know what you've done, Father.

I open the last door to the right of the right fork and find a man inside wearing a dust mask. He's whittling a stick. Next to him is a tigress, her paw mangled in a trap. The meters behind her are ticking louder as she weakens. The masked man continues whittling his stick, whistling as he works. He stares through me and looks bored. The tree door is occupied by a jungle owlet, a monitor lizard, and a sleepy langur mother with her baby. Spotted deer glance in, alerted by tiger moans.

When the tigress is too weak to hold her head up, the man jabs his stick through her mouth into her throat. She can no longer make tiger-music; the forest guard won't hear her as the man batters her spine. He gets out his skinning knife and slits her down the front. Half an hour it takes him to flay her. Then he wipes his hands and sits on the ground to eat his breakfast on a teak leaf, before digging a hole to bury the flesh and tiger bones to retrieve later. He creeps out of the forest with her pelt.

Father, I have learnt to be quiet as a tree, so quiet even the monkeys come and sleep on me. I am a door no one can open. When I went to live with my grandmother, she told me stories about the jungle. I put all her creatures in the cellar, so I could fall asleep at night. Every time I was locked in, they were there waiting for me. Thirty-four years I survived with her animals' help. Then you reappeared and I realised the animals were wounded, many dead, their skins ripped off, their bones pulled out and sold in the market.

2

By my fortieth birthday I was nothing but boneless meat buried in the ground. No one could piece me together.

Then my grandmother told me the story of meeting a tiger when she was a baby. She had been placed in a tent in the jungle and left alone. She remembered seeing the fiery creature enter the tent and approach her cot, but she hadn't been afraid. She'd held out her hand and touched its fur. It looked down at her, then went back out. That was when I decided to go to India and see tigers for myself, to try to get up close as she had done.

Father, let me tell you what I saw. Come with me, I am at the gate of Tala Zone, the core of Bandhavgarh. You are long dead now. Hundreds of tigers have been poached. I want to understand why anyone would harm them. I want to understand why you harmed me. I go into the park alone, at night, night after night. I watch the poachers at work. I see them set their traps, their snares, and hide their skinning knives under a rock.

But I have also seen Bheem, with his cleft nose and battle eye, his sunrise-striped hulk, as he lies cooling in the stream. I have seen a treepie pick the scraps from between his teeth. I have seen a doe carrying a langur on her back when the monkey was drunk on mahua flowers. I have seen a vine snake steal the eggs from weaver nests – they hung from the tree of life like teardrops. I have seen the Indian roller in flight, the azure skies and lapis seas of his wings! I have seen the tailorbird sewing two leaves into a nest.

I have seen the paradise flycatcher! I have seen his midnight-blue face, his ice-crystal tail streamers trailing through the branches of burning trees, and he did not melt, even though the brainfever bird called, while the temperature soared. I have heard the cicadas singing to fever pitch as the monsoon breaks. And yet the paradise bird flew, trailing his snowflakes like windows in a nursery hung with silver chimes. I have seen him flying like the last winter on Earth.

I have walked in full moonlight, in the tracks of Bhitri as she hunts. I have stood at the rim of her ravine as she emerges in the cool of sunset. I have heard the monkeys bark a warning from the treetops, the chitals' high-pitched calls echoing all around me, the sambars' plosive alerts in the forest-theatre. I have come face to face with the huntress. I have seen her eyes trying to escape their confines, the pupils darting back and forth in their orbits. Then I have followed her home, back to her ravine cave, and heard her cracking the bones of her fawn. I was cunning as Bhitri, whose name means 'innermost jungle'.

Listen! If you are good, you'll see what she sees – the air quivering with scented paths into the perfumed forest. You'll hear the vulture rapture on Rajbhera Meadow, the snuffle of jackals as they gather. Come with me to the feast. Bandhavgarh Fort shimmers in the background, its cliffs laced with griffon nests. And here, halfway up the plateau, lies Vishnu, surrounded by cobras.

I have heard the trees of light and the trees of darkness whispering to each other, their leaves shaking like tiny maracas. I have made friends with every door, every tree in the forest – even the tree of secrets, the one a leopard lies in. She has dragged you up to a lightning fork, where she licks your face as if to wash you.

IV

What Rough Beast?

I asked if I could leave the Earth

but no one answered.
I looked in the mirror and one side of my face
was fighting the other side.
My mouth was a pit into which they threw the dead,
my teeth the rubble of bombed buildings.
There was a word for what was wrong with me
but no word for the troubles on Earth.
I saw that my lashes were barbed wires
that would cut anyone who looked into my eyes,
my eyes that pleaded to escape.

A Mother Sings

I have tucked my daughter back
into my womb.

I have taken her through my Red Sea.
Bomb blasts are muffled there.

She no longer has to breathe poisonous air.
She is cushioned from shrapnel.

She doesn't have to run on premature legs.
Her lungs are tamarisks where doves perch.

My breasts prepare her milk and honey.
They sing to her of paradise.

I will rebirth her on banks of the river of life.
I'll wade through the river of thorns

while she still sleeps.
I am her country and her lagoon.

I've draped my bones with hanging gardens
for her to crawl into when she arrives.

What Eagle Saw

Eagle looked down and with her laser vision
zoomed into the neonatal clinic.

Her third eyelids closed against the smashed incubators
but her eyes kept looking.
She saw into the chests of newborns
where the twigs of lungs were torn.

She saw the buds of burst gardens.
She saw the roses of hearts open,
she saw the worms feeding inside
where the pollen of life had bloomed.

She saw the rivers of veins dry up.
She saw the deserts of new skins crack
and out of the cracks crawled scorpions.

She saw the roots of unready eyes
detonate like fuse wires.

Eagle called for the doves to come
with olive branches in their beaks, she asked
for an armistice between all the birds.

She flew far off, but couldn't erase what she had seen.

Butcherbirds

Hope may nest, its inkwell mean more than any grail
when a Palestine sunbird lines her home with down

from an angel's fontanelle. When, instead of bombs,
white storks land on roofs and build their nests

from salvaged olive sprigs, while in the burnt groves
a dove finds one green vowel. Even the raven brings his gift

of holy quills when the soldiers come, showers them
with stardust from his feathers, so they see their humanity

and harm no one. I watch all this with barbed wire lashes –
on each spike a shrike has impaled hope. Yet

I know that sparrows nest under a stork's eyrie,
keep mosquitoes of shrapnel from their hosts' chicks.

The commonest bird can be the most lyrical, when
she perches on a warhead that hatches only song.

Salt Bride

(after Sigalit Landau)

How long has Earth floated in her salt dress?
When did her bridal gown crystallise,

weighing her down like an anchor
inside a dead sea?

Who lowered her into the abyss?
Whose tears does she wear?

Bride who once somersaulted
through the fathoms like a song-whale

flooding ships with her psalms,
homing through the deep,

attended by shoals of stars.
She is an antique dress

with crinoline hoops
encrusted with islands and continents.

Lonely blue-white jewel,
no fish to stroke her plastic bags

snagged inside the lace
where once she had a body.

Beauty

When Beauty woke from her hundred-year sleep
        the birds had all gone. She saw that she was covered

in brambles and abandoned nests. She shrugged off
        her dress that had turned to dust and stood up in her glass coffin.

She saw that her stepmother was dead, her father too was
        dead, but she was still alive and young. She started searching

for princes but they too were dead. She was all alone
        in her silver forest. If she pricked herself on a thorn the wound

healed. If she ate a rotten apple she knew which leaves to chew
        to neutralise the poison. She walked about naked.

When Beauty woke from her coma the palace was a ruin
        and all the rose trees flowered only for her.

She gathered their thorny stems and made herself a
        barrier against the sun's rays and the stars that kept

flowering in the sky, trying to land in her world.
        She looked at the moon and saw it was a mirror, her face

the colour of rain. Her lips were white roses she'd plucked
        for her father. Beast was a shadow face behind hers,

like an eclipse. Am I the last human on Earth? she asked
        her reflection, and the moon answered

that she was a fairytale which had woken. Her hair was
        silver so she wondered if she was old even though her

features were young. You are a memento of fertility
        the moon replied, once upon a time you were green.

V

Beast of Bodmin

(Bodmin Moor, Cornwall)

The Moor Horses

We race from the top of Kilmar Tor
to see them gallop across the plateau, manes flying, tails

streaming behind, as they plunge into the water
and stand there cooling while foals roll on the grass.

And still the horses arrive, as if they've descended
from petroglyphs, released from millennia carved on walls,

tracing the water-scent, the ancestral map to this pool
set in the slope like a gem-framed black mirror.

They are frost and flint hooved, the appaloosa stallion
splashed with sparks from bonfires in the great caverns.

His mare erupts from the mud
and glares at us, her eyes dusted with rock sleep.

Hasn't she just woken from stone dreams? Doesn't her pearl coat
with its bronze paint tell us she is sacred?

And isn't your blood free as a feral pony, coursing
through the uplands of your body? Your bones granite,

your marrow clear as the brooks that thread down to the valleys.
The months that we trekked up through the ruins

and you photographed each stonechat and lark,
our picnics under fruiting rowans, then up

to the top of the tor, with its stone formations
like fertility goddesses. And that last hot day when

the horses appeared, and flew beneath Bearah Tor.
Their blessing, when the whole moor raised itself to the sky

like a shield to protect us. That moment when you
held out your hand and touched the stallion – as if you too

were made of porphyry and quartz that had just sprung to life.

Galloway Bull at the Waterhole

The black bull growled like an earthquake,
he pawed the ground and glared.

I retreated to a rock to eat my picnic,
the waterhole belonged to him
and his banded cows as they bathed.

The black bull looked like he was made
of thunder and black ice,
his shaggy coat heavy as midnight.

His balls hung in their sacs like rain clouds
about to burst, his pizzle a lightning bolt.

The moor swung around him like a cloak,
its stunted haws and gorse fur clotted with sheep.

I left so long ago, ran from the wild,
but that bull is still there at the back of my mind,

my mind that's a moor now, scratching me as I pass,
its cobwebs tearing like my mother's thighs

the day I was born. I don't know which gate
I left by, which stony bridle path
I've trudged all my life, searching for him.

Did the ravens up on the tor
carry me off, never to return to earth's maze?

The bull's face with its galaxies of flies!
His eyes were the wolf moon and its twin in black water

and his tail that he swished, dripping mud,
was the tail of the universe – hot and angry.

Roebuck

(Poem beginning with a line by Lucie Brock-Broido)

Tell me there is a meadow, afterwards,
that the roebuck will come
to the top of my garden,

that the window will cut me
with glass blades
of dewy hooves.

That I'll lay out my doe mask,
my necklace of icicles,
onto the deep windowsill.

Tell me the buck will be there
among nettles and briar, his mouth
panting, his lungs clear.

That his legs won't tangle
in the electric wire
around my tower.

That if he can't find his way
back into the before,
his horns jewelled

with thorns and flowers
might grow into a tall grove.
Tell me that even in my solitude,

my altar goods laid out
to the god of woods,
that this red buck

against the steep viridian field
will sprout a ladder between his tines
that I can climb.

That his antlers will be strong
as my spine, that I will scale
the rungs of myself

out onto the clouded
chancel of the sky, my body
slick as a newborn fawn.

Ode to a Cornish Hedge

Thousand-mile-long rainforest, shaggy remnant, where I slow to hear air
pass through earwig spiracles, and bumblebees are thunder-loud in foxgloves.

I walk along you, peering down fox-runs. Or I lean in, towards your
prehistoric core – slate and granite years, jewel matrix of earth's dreams

whispered by worms, spider spun maps to stars. I try to translate
hieroglyphs of soil, your root-nets where hedgelings call.

The first day is always prising your velvets open. I love to plunge my fingers in,
I love to be at the brim of danger, canticles of croziers unfurling spiral

nebulae. I never know what discoveries will come, what leopard-
spotted orchids, what bryonies, bat hammocks under hazel!

You're surface scripted too – red campioned, bluebell belfried, buttercup gilded
pictograms. Stitchwort, dog violet, willowherb, and blackthorn over-storeyed.

And above these – canopy giants of oak, ash, beech, bark legs of gods,
their faces wreathed in cloud, attended by jays, buzzards,

wood pigeons, woodpeckers. Gods encaged in ivy buttresses.
Let me be in earth's childhood again, a hedgehoglet.

Let me roll myself back to the rain eras.
Let me remember the clear songs of rain as it blessed the first ferns.

Here under the organ pipe stems, as sunlight filters through clerestories
and the blackbird's clarion is a welcome. The dunnocks chat

as if I've been in their nurseries since birth. Everything is bower-cot.
Let the nurses try to pick my lice scabs! I'll scratch them

with bramble fingers, sting them with nettle hairs. You've heard of children
raised by wolves? I was raised by weasels and treecreepers.

My playmates were toads and lizards. Whenever I needed help,
I came to the hedge, and it listened. Even now I hear its voices soft as moss,

wildflowers speaking through light. I drank honeydew and fed on dung.
I saw the grass snake curled under straw like an unanswerable question.

I saw colours birds see – ultraviolent infra-bloods.
And when I had to leave the hedge, its spirit followed me like a thousand-mile

shadow, a god-snake with trees growing from its spine, feathered serpent
the field mice whisper codes to and owls screech morse until I am a hedge-hide

again and the adults are erased. I speak moth. I turn myself into a hoverfly
and crawl on the ceiling. With my compound eyes I can predict

where the hand will hit. The hedge is my tail as I enter the orphanage.
Hail, Cornish hedge, trembling as the tractor nears, survivor who bears the flail!

Song Thrush

We only see him through binoculars –
the way we view life
beyond lockdown, blurry,
its beak open.

Does he sing about the snow moon
during our winter twilight?
He does not spare his breath
or his heart

which seems about to burst.
He does not spare his lungs.
If his life is shortened by his melody
he sings louder.

He sings as if he will die
when his aria is over.
I don't think he notices us, even though
we pass through the gate

to see who is up there, silhouetted
at the top of the bare tree.
A car passes and he continues,
singing everything he knows,

as if he wants to sing of fumes
and smoke. Even viruses
can be changed into notes.
Just as some of us sang

on balconies to join in operas
and violin concertos
or just bang spoons against a pan
as if to ward off demons.

Does he sing about the nest
his mate is building
from mud and sticks?
Or the eggs she will lay

blue as new worlds?
His eye is dark as the night sky
on the tree of heaven. He perches
as we are perched, on an outer branch

of the Milky Way. And perhaps
that is singing too,
and we are just a spark
in the universe's eye.

Swallows

Your forked tails are calligraphy brushes
writing me letters on air
with gliding seeds and clouds of gnats,

while the earth keeps flying,
never stopping to build a nest.

I keep asking you for answers,
what is the language of home? I ask.

Mud, you sing, and you me show me a grass stem
trailing roots from a clod.

And I see our planet migrating through space
like you my summer visitors –

the Saharas of your undersides!
The red mountains of your faces!
The moonlit nights of your wings!

You sing about shoals of flying fish
and your eyes glitter with seas.

Your speech is more like a sigh
or the creak of a sail on the deep.

I can't sit still. My shoulders ache
as if I've been flying for weeks.

I think about hanging upside-down from the ceiling,
even my windows open their beaks.

I gather white feathers that float down
like summer snowflakes from your beam.
My fingers grip the pen like an overhead wire.

What is this letter I'm writing on paper
new as a fledgling's breast?

What are these insects I feed my pages?

Murmurations at Roughtor

When I think of us, I hear the clap of wings,
    the way the starlings pass over and over,

        the white plops on our shoulders
            as if they want us to wear their disguise

of a convict's arrowed pyjamas
    or paint us with heavens of stars

        before the smoky ballets drawn
            by charcoal bodies on air.

When I think of us, we are shivering
    high up on the moor as late arrivals

        snake in and explode. They could be
            a plague of hungry beaked angels

watching our tilted faces turn orange
    in sunset, the mackerel clouds on fire.

        And every scene from our lives flies here
            tucked with the birds into pines –

all our days flown in to roost.
    Roughtor sleeps after millennia

        guarding the moor. Even
            the forest roosts, its firs lying

on the ground as if asleep. When I think of us
    stripped by a searing wind,

        we are starlings nestled on branches,
            our throats quivering with snores.

Beast of Bodmin

You say I don't exist, that the panther skull you found
in the river is fake, my alien origins
betrayed by an Indian cockroach egg-case
nestled like a ruby in my brain.

You say that walkers have heard me howl as if caught
in a trap or calling for a mate. That I escaped
from a private estate where I grew too dangerous to keep,
that I kill sheep by skinning them face-first.

That I could be pure myth – the Butterfly-Jaguar
with eyespots on my wings to frighten off humans,
that I wear a pelt of moon-moths by night.

~

Few have found my pugmarks, but they are homes to vanishing insects.

You see no gouges on the rowans,
but my claws are gorse where stonechats nest

and the spaces between my paws are tussocks
where skylarks hatch.

Each of my hairs is a recording of birdsong.

~

Sometimes you glimpse me crouched on a lightning fork,
my roar thundering downhill.

You say my face is vast as the moorland sky,
that a raincloud parts
to give me eyes that glow in the dark.

You call me beast, but I am the hazel and oak woods
that once costumed the moor,
my veins streams that feed the valleys.

My yawn is the shaggy mists of sunrise,
my spit the lichen rags on trees.

~

I emerged from the swamp like a newly-cast mirror,
my rosettes barely visible in peat fur.

I am the curator of my own heaven
hung with paintings of starry nights
that whirl on my glossy coat.

My rosettes are not your quarries or mines
but the roses of pulsars, medals from eco-wars!

Yet all you see are rail-holes in granite sleepers of disused railways.

Extinct plants flex their colours when I run!

~

I pass through the understorey of the ghost-forest
like a photo in the developer tray, a shadow printed
with earth's apex language.
Yet you scan snaps of me and say they're forged.

I am the codex of unnamed species, the librarian of lost trees.

I am written in rare fonts of ambrosial inks,
in bog asphodels and heath orchids, marsh violets and sundew.
My belly is plush as sphagnum.
My ears are cists and cairns.

My breath is the wind that whips your face
and cradles the kestrel.

~

My heart is set in the slope like a reed-framed waterhole.

When the feral ponies come to bathe in me
I make them new as cave paintings that have just sprung to life.

My glance is the sheen on the stallion's silver coat,
the spots that mark him as a leopard-horse!

His mare bursts from the surface, her eyes blazing,
her bracken coat streaked with amnion.

~

You say I don't exist, but my bones are old as granite,
my marrow clear as the brooks that tumble
down to the valleys. My flesh is feldspar and quartz,
my tail is hoarfrost and fern flame.

~

You say I never existed, but my ancestors once roamed these heights,
their fangs became icicles dripping from cheesewrings,
their fur melted like a drift.

I could be stem cells
in the vial of a Frozen Zoo, waiting
a hundred years to awake

in my city of glass towers,
my smoking biobank.
I could be an immortal leopard

in a deep-frozen forest, surrounded by
lynx, wolf, deer – all of us dreaming
of a new Ice Age to cool the earth.

ACKNOWLEDGEMENTS

My thanks to the editors of the following publications, where some of these poems were first published, sometimes in other versions: *The Aftershock Review, bath magg, Butcher's Dog, Cornish Modern Poetries* (Broken Sleep Books, 2022), *Count Every Breath* (Hawakal, India, 2023), *Dancing about Architecture* (MadHat, Inc., US, 2024), *Festival in a Book: A Celebration of Wenlock Poetry Festival* (Wenlock Poetry Festival, 2023), *Granta, Magma, The Manhattan Review* (US), *Modron, New Humanist, The North, Planet, Poetry* (US), *Poetry: A Writer's Guide and Anthology* (Bloomsbury Academic, US, 2023), *Poetry London, The Poetry Review, Quay Voices #2: New Writing from Quay Words at Exeter Custom House 2021-2022* (Literature Works, 2022), *The Rialto, The Stinging Fly, Ten Poems from Cornwall* (Candlestick Press, 2023), *The Times Literary Supplement, Versus Versus: 100 Poems by Deaf, Disabled & Neurodivergent Poets* (Bloodaxe Books, 2025), *Verse Daily* and *Vox Populi* (US).

Thank you to Cornwall AONB who commissioned 'Beast of Bodmin' as an extra award on my winning the inaugural Laurel Prize in 2020 for *Mama Amazonica*. I'm indebted to William Atkins for commissioning 'Tala Zone' for *Granta* 157: *Should We Have Stayed at Home? New Travel Writing*, and for his guest editing. Thank you to BBC Radio 4's *The Verb* for commissioning 'Swallows' for their *Something New* series, and for featuring my poem 'Civet de Cerf'. Thank you to editors Jacqueline Saphra and Andy Jackson for commissioning 'Peace Sonnet #6', now titled 'Butcherbirds' here in *Beast*, for their *Peace Sonnet Chain* (Whaleback City Press, 2024). My peace sonnet first appeared online in *New Boots and Pantisocracies*, thanks W.N. Herbert for encouragement for this commission. Thank you Fiona Benson, whose prompts provided first drafts for 'Dumbo Octopus' and 'Beauty', in her workshop during our co-tutored Tŷ Newydd course, 'Metaphor and Metamorphosis', in August 2024. 'The Beast of Vaccarès' owes its story to Jousè d'Arbaud's *The Beast and Other Tales* (Northwestern University Press, 2020), translated from Provençal by Joyce Zonana.

Three of the poems in *Beast* owe lines to other poets, and are homages. 'Hide (Emperors and Egrets)' begins with a line from John Burnside's poem 'Loved and Lost' from his collection *Black Cat Bone* (Cape, 2011). 'Ode to the Camargue' has an epigraph quoting lines from Pablo Neruda's *Canto General* (University of California Press, 1991), translated by Jack Schmitt. 'Roebuck' begins with a line which ends Lucie Brock-Broido's poem 'A Meadow' from her collection *Stay, Illusion* (Random House Inc, 2013). Her last couplet is: 'Tell me there is / A meadow, afterward.'

I would like to thank Maria Lucia Santoro, the daughter of the artist Eugenio Santoro, for permission to grace my cover with her father's sculpture, *Sans titre* (*c*. 2000), Collection de l'Art Brut, Lausanne (Suisse). Thank you Neil Astley and Pamela Robertson-Pearce for the striking cover design from my photos of Eugenio Santoro's sculpture. Many thanks to Vincent Monod for permission to use this work from the Collection de l'Art Brut, and to Rachel Falconer who took me to this extraordinary museum where I found the face of my *Beast*.

I am enormously grateful to the Royal Literary Fund for financial support, which enabled me to write the first part of *Beast*. I would like to thank the Society of Authors for their Arthur Welton Award for this collection while in progress, which allowed me to spend time in the Camargue and complete the manuscript. I would also like to thank them for financial support during Covid.

A special thank you to my editor Neil Astley, for his dedication, encouragement and editing, and to all the wonderful people at Bloodaxe. Finally, thank you to my husband and first reader, Brian Fraser, for his invaluable comments on the poems.

EU DECLARATION OF GPSR CONFORMITY

Books published by Bloodaxe Books are identified by the EAN/ISBN printed above our address on the copyright page and manufactured by the printer whose address is noted below. This declaration of conformity is issued under the sole responsibility of the publisher, the object of declaration being each individual book produced in conformity with the relevant EU harmonisation legislation with no known hazards or warnings, and is made on behalf of Bloodaxe Books Ltd on 24 April 2025 by Neil Astley, Managing Director, editor@bloodaxebooks.com.